Around the World Series

ROMANIA: BOOK THREE

BY JAMIE PEDRAZZOLI

I want to thank my Mother Jane Pedrazzoli for coloring all the drawings in this book so they can brighten up the pages.

Copyright 2018 © Jamie Pedrazzoli, also known as Jamie Bach

Copyright fuels creativity. Thank you for buying an authorized edition of this book and complying with the copyright laws by not reproducing, scanning, or distributing any part of this book in any form without permission. To contact the author for permissions email pedrazzolij@yahoo.com.

ISBN-13: 978-1721270996

ISBN-10: 172127099X

The names in this book are used fictitiously and any resemblance of persons is coincidental. The facts in this book are based on information provided to the author.

Buna (Boo-Nah), or Hello. Numele meu este Lavinia Marinescu (New-mel-ay May Es-tay Lah-vin-ee-ah Mar-en-es-koo) or My name is Lavinia Marinescu. I am from the County Romania. Have you heard of it? Romania is located in Eastern Europe. We have Ukraine to the North, Moldova to the East, Serbia, Bulgaria and the Black Sea are to the South, and Hungary is to the West.

This is the shape of my country.

Why don't I tell you a little about what to do in the Capital City of Bucharest, where I live?

A major building that tourists like to visit is the World's largest Administrative Building. It was built in 1997 and is known as the Palace of Parliament. There are over 1,100 rooms inside this massive building and it is twelve stories tall!

The photo below is downtown Bucharest.

We have art and science museums. We have theaters that perform plays and operas.

There is a village museum here that has replicas of old buildings from the 1600 and 1900s! I love this museum. I like to walk around them and imagine I was living during that time.

There is so much to do and see in Romania! There are beaches, mountain trails, natural springs, spas, vineyards, medieval towns, and castles.

We have all kinds of transportation that can be seen here in the city. We have buses, trains, bicycles, boats,

and donkey drawn carts.

Now I want to tell you some quick information about my country.

The Capitol city is Bucharest. The estimated population in 2017 was 19,580,634 people. Our major religion is Christianity. The major language we speak is Romanian. However Hungarian, Turkish, German, Albanian, Romani, and English are spoken as well.

Our National flower is the Dog Rose.

Our National animal is the Lynx.

The National bird is the Great White Pelican and the Golden Eagle.

The money here is called the Leu. One hundred Romanian RON equals about $25 USD. The average monthly salary is 2,360 RON or $630 USD. Only 25 % of Romanians own a television. Only 15 % can afford a car.

Football (soccer) is the most popular sport in Romania. Other sports that many enjoy are volleyball, basketball, rugby, tennis, and gymnastics.

Romania is the 9th largest wine producer in the world.

The Danube is the main river in Romania. It flows from the West to the East and out into the Black Sea.

A very exciting place to visit is the Scărișoara Cave; it is the biggest underground glacier in Romania and the second largest underground glacier in South-Eastern Europe. This Ice Cave is found on the premises of Apuseni Natural Park underneath the Bihor Mountains.

Another natural beauty is the Bigar Waterfall. It is located in the Caras-Severin County in the Western part of Romania; the amazing Bigar Waterfall is called "the miracle from the Minis Canyon" by the locals. This waterfall resembles a mushroom that has water flowing around it. It reminds me of something in a fairytale story. It is truly a one of a kind waterfall. Nowhere else in the world will you find one that looks like this!

The Peleș Castle was the first European castle entirely lit by electric current! The castle had its own electrical plant that let it have a heating system. This was built in 1888 in Sinala and is still functioning today! It is considered the masterpiece of Renaissance architecture.

The only Gold Museum in Europe is found in Brad Romania. The Gold museum contains a collection of over 2,000 exhibits gathered from all around the world. Some of the museum's exhibits are made of

native gold found in the local Metaliferi Mountains.

The Ice Hotel is near the Fagarass range of the Carpathians, among the highest peaks in Romania, and is accessible only by cable car. Rooms are made entirely from ice! Would you stay in a hotel made from ice?

The Berca Muddy Volcanoes are a tourist's delight! The muddy volcanoes are formed due to underground eruptions of gases generated by deep oilfields. The gas released by the black oil magma penetrates through crevices and fissures, and spits out mud with smoke! These are a rare sight in our world.

We have about 2, 500 lakes in Romania. Our climate is humid, cold, and damp in the mountainous regions.

Our spring is short with a lot of rain. This sometimes causes areas along the Danube River to flood! The average temperature in the summer is 73 Degrees Fahrenheit or 23 Degrees Celsius.

In the winter it's around 27 Degrees Fahrenheit or negative 3 Degrees Celsius! Is that too cold for you?

My country is very green. It is full of rolling hills and mountains. We have about ¼ of the country covered in forests. Common trees in these forests are oak and beech.

Can you guess some of the animals that live here in our forest and mountainous regions? There are over 400 mammals that live in my country.

Some of those are foxes, wolves, lynxes, wild pigs, and bears.

We also have a rare animal called the Chamois (Sha-Mee) that roams the mountains. It is similar in appearance to a goat.

There are a lot of birds and fish as well near the Danube River.

We have over a dozen Natural Reservations and more than 100 parks to help preserve the wildlife. What is your favorite animal?

At least 60 % of our land is farmland and we rely on tourism to help support our economy. Some of the agricultural things we grow are wheat, corn, barley, beets, sunflower seeds, potatoes, and grapes. We also raise sheep, cattle, horses, and pigs.

We export lumber, cement, clothing, and shoes. We manufacture steel, iron, textiles, chemicals, construction materials, and gold.

 This is the Romanian flag. The blue stands for liberty, the yellow stands for justice, and the red stands for fraternity, which means people sharing a common interest.

This is a photo of the Carpathian Mountains.

Thanks for listening to me speak about Romania. La revedere (lah-rev-ve-day-ray) or Goodbye.

Buna, Numele meu este Alexandru Melosovici, or Hello, My name is Alexandru Melosovici. I live in a small rural village called Patrahaitesti (Pat-tra-hi-es-tee). Tourists come to see the many waterfalls we have here and to learn about traditional Romania.

My cousin Vlad is wearing the traditional Romanian apparel with my sister Andreea. Romanian boys wear long white pants, white shirts, and black vests that are sometimes striped with red and gold. They also wear a black hat.

Girls' usually wear white shirts, black vests with red and gold embroidered designs, and striped aprons over a white skirt. They also wear decorated scarves over their hair.

The rural areas are known for their artistic abilities such as fancy embrodery, costumes, colorful rugs, painted easter eggs, painted glass, and decorative plates.

Since we live in a small village we know everyone in town. I have many chores to do each

day to help my family. Early morning before school I milk our cows and feed our chickens. I bring the chicken eggs inside and my mother prepares breakfast.

I want to tell you a little about some traditional dances.

The dance called the Hora is a traditional Romanian folk dance where the dancers hold each other's hands and the circle spins, usually counterclockwise, as each participant follows a sequence of three steps forward and one step back. The dance is usually accompanied by musical instruments such as the accordion, violin, saxophone, and the trumpet or pan pipes. I perform this dance a lot at festivals or weddings with other friends and family. It is very fun and entertaining to us as well as tourists.

Romania is a very superstitious country. The Government today has a black magic tax on witches and fortune tellers! False predictions can result in fines! Now I will tell you about a magical dance.

The Calusari are described as a group of men, sworn to stay together in ritual dancing for a period of nine years. Their secrets are never told. They are feared warriors who fight the "Iele" which means, Mythical fairies.

The origins of the Calusari are unknown. Although the oath taken is made in the name of God, the mythical ritual enacted by the Calusari has nothing in common with Christianity.

The Calusari have to stay together for the sworn period to remain invulnerable and invested with supernatural powers, if they break away from the group they will fall prey to the Iele. Together, they are stronger.

The dance of the Calusari has different functions through spells performed during the dance. They believe the benefits to this ritual are speeding up marriage and fertility of the young women who join at the end of the dance, healing the sick, and sending away the Iele through the practice of warrior acts, and the use of magical plants during the dance. The Calusari dance is considered one of the fastest and most spectacular dances in the world. Today it is mostly performed for fun and for tourists to enjoy.

Since we are on the subject of magic and superstitions, have you heard of Dracula? Dracula is a Vampire! Though Dracula is purely a made up creation, *Author Bram Stoker* named his character after a real person who happened to have a taste for blood: Vlad III, Prince of Wallachia or, Vlad the Impaler. The nickname is a demonstration of the prince's favorite way to dispense his enemies.

Other than having the same name, the two Draculas' don't really have much in common, according to historians who have studied them.

Vlad Dracula's castle is called Bran Castle; the fortress is situated on the border between Transylvania and Wallachia and is a popular tourist attraction today.

Another book that was written about this castle is called "The Castle in the Carpathians", by *Jules Verne.*

How about learning some Romanian history?

In 800 B.C. the Dacians settled in the Transylvanian region of Romania. The Dacians farmed and traded.

Dacian King Decebel is carved into a rock on the bank of the Danube River and is the tallest rock sculpture in Europe.

In A.D 107 the Romans conquered the Dacians.

In the 1300's two independent regions are formed. One is called Moldovia and one is called Walachia.

In 1861 the two regions unite.

In 1866 King Carol I served as Romania's first king. Later his son Michael became king.

In 1881 Romania became a Kingdom.

In 1916 and 1944 Romania fought in both World Wars.

In 1947 the Soviet Union takes control over Romania.

In 1965 Romania declares itself independent from the Soviet Union.

In 1980 Romania faced hard economic times. There was a food shortage.

In 1990 free elections are held and people are able to vote! They vote in Ion Iliescu for President.

In 1991 the constitution is adopted.

In 2007 Romania joined the EU or European Union.

 This is a picture of the tunnel of love, it is an abandoned train track overgrown with stunning trees. This is a beautiful place for photographs.

Now I want to talk to you a little about school. School is free for Romanian children ages 6 to 16. We spend 8 years in elementary school. English is taught in some schools. Secondary schools often teach a trade such as teaching, art, or technical skills that can be used on the job. Top graduates from the class often prepare for college. There are 7 popular universities in Romania.

One of my favorite things is food! What is your favorite food?

A typical Romanian breakfast includes eggs, bread, cheese, and coffee. Lunch is usually a light meal such as soup. Dinner is big and usually includes meat, veggies, and potatoes.

Cabbage pancakes are a popular breakfast food. Would you eat a cabbage pancake?

Mitiei (mee-tea-tay) are cylinder shaped meatballs.

Sarmale (sar-mah-lay) Cabbage Rolls

Mamaliga (mah-mah-lee-gah) is cornmeal mush usually served as mashed potatoes.

Pastries are a delicious and common dessert!

Tzucia (tsoo-ee-kuh) or plum brandy is a popular drink for adults.

This is the Coat of Arms.

Before I go, I want to talk a little about the Romanian government. We have a legislative parliament made of Deputies and Senators. There are 332 seats in the Chamber and 137 in the Senate.

At 18 years of age you can vote. We appoint members with these popular votes.

We have Judicial, Supreme, County Local, and Military Courts. Communism ended in 1989 and in 1991 Romania became a Republic.

Thanks for listening to me. I hope you learned something.

Sastipe (sas-tea-pay) or Hello, Lachho Dives (lach-ho-Dives) or Good Day, My name is Isadora Lee and I am a Roma or gypsy from Romania. I speak Romani or Rromanës which is different from Romanian. There are about an estimated 5% Roma living in Romania.

The Roma originated from Northern India. Our language is more common with Hindi and Punjabi than it is with the Romanian language. The Roma people face discrimination because of our dark skin and we were once enslaved by Europeans. In 1554, the English Parliament passed a law that made being a Gypsy a felony. The Roma have been portrayed as cunning, mysterious outsiders who tell fortunes and steal before moving on to the next town. The term "gypped" is probably an abbreviation of Gypsy, meaning someone who is sly. We do not like this term. As a matter of survival we were always on the move.

Some Roma are citizens of Romania but most Roma in Europe have no connection whatsoever with Romania.

My people live by a set of rules that govern things such as cleanliness, purity, respect, and justice and these rules are referred to as "Rromano."

We have adopted the religions where we live; we Roma do not have our own religion.

My people are discriminated against even in today's times and many endure hate crimes. This is a sad situation but there are many people in Romania trying to help.

Enough of that talk let me tell you about something happy. I want to tell you about Romanian holidays!

Romanian people celebrate both Easter and Christmas.

December 1ˢᵗ National Day is celebrated. It is also called Great Union Day.

On March 1ˢᵗ Mărțișor is celebrated. Men give woman and girls small brooches.

Children's Day (*Ziua Copilului*) is a national holiday celebrated in Romania. It is held on June 1 every year. Teachers give certificates, communities display children's art work, and some families have big dinners.

In July in Bucharest there is a celebration with a parade where people wear clothing from the 1800's. They do this to remember the old traditions. Traditional music and food is also enjoyed on this day.

In rural areas on the 3ʳᵈ Sunday in July single men and woman attend a maiden's fair where they dance and feast as they look for a husband or wife.

In August there is a dance at Prislop pass in the Carpathian Mountains where traditional clothing is worn and there is a feast and celebration. This is to celebrate the connection of Translyvania, Moldova, and Maramures.

Also in August is the Folk Art Festival where many crafts are displayed.

Sambra Oilor is in autumn and marks the return of the sheep herds from the mountains.

There are also wine festivals to celebrate the grape harvest.

Romanians like any excuse to gather with friends and families to celebrate.

I want to leave you with some famous Romanian people.

Constantin Brâncușiis is one of the best sculptors in the world. He is known for the Table of Silence and the Endless Column. He carves elegant shapes from wood and marble.

Iancu Văcărescu is known as the father of Romanian poetry.

Nadia Comaneci at age 14 in the 1976 Olympics scored the first perfect 10 in the history of Olympic gymnastics. Many Romanian girls want to be gymnasts and there is a large Olympic training center in Deva Romania where the national gymnastics team is taught today.

Béla Károlyi was Nadia's coach and is known throughout the world as one of the best coaches in woman's gymnastics.

Thank you for taking the time to read our stories about Romania. I will leave you with some phrases from the Romani language.

Sar San? (Sahr-sahn) How are you?

Mishto, palikerav tut (meesh-toe-pah-lee-ker-ave-toot)

Fine, thank you.

Sar si sogadi (sahr-see-so-gah-dee) How is everything?

Kanchi (kahn-chee) Nothing.

Miro Nav si o …(your name) (Mer-row Nahv-see-oh …) My name is ….

Dja devlesa (Djya-Dev-less-uh) Goodbye.

 This is a picture of the National Gymnastics training center in Deva Romania.

The End.

Thank you for taking the time to read my Third book in the 'Around the World' Series. Book four will be about the country of Costa Rica! I hope to do many more countries in the near future. If you live in a foreign country and would like to send me facts about your country and a list of holidays it would be welcomed. Just contact the author at pedrazzolij@yahoo.com.

I wanted to share the cultures of the world with young generations, which is why I chose to start this series. I have always loved and respected people and places from around the world. I hope these books will teach others about how different yet how small our world really is.

The Around the World Series includes:

Book One: Denmark

Book Two: India

Please support me as an author by checking out my other books available under Jamie Bach. My books can be purchased online at most online bookstores.

Other books available include

For kids and young adults

Tongue twisting alphabet fun with Koby Jack and Bogart

Counting shapes and color fun with Koby Jack and Bogart

My jungle adventure in Costa Rica

Jess the Fox (also in Spanish) Jess el Zorro

Florida girls

Florida girls 2

Let's learn site words Kindergarten

Books For Adults or Teens

Aleida Orphan no more a Cinderella story with a twist

Words of encouragement and how to cope with what life brings you

Untrusting Eyes

School for the Enchanted

About the Author

Jamie Pedrazzoli (Jamie Bach) grew up in Vero Beach Florida where she spent time taking art classes in high school with the Center for the Arts Museum. She always enjoyed reading and writing.

She has two daughters that help inspire her to write.

"I'm so glad to be able to share my books with the world, I hope everyone enjoys reading them" she says.

Check out her websites and other links to social media.

Amazon site

http://www.amazon.com/Jamie-Bach/e/B00LP37ZK4

Author site on facebook

https://www.facebook.com/jamiebachauthorchildrensbooks

Author site

http://authorjamiebach.weebly.com

Twitter

https://twitter.com/jamiebach421

Adventure Blog

http://theadventuresofkobyjackandbogart.weebly.com

Remember if you wish to contact this author an email address is provided. Do not call her or her parents' home. This is an invasion of privacy and is not appreciated. If it is of urgent importance EMAIL is the best way.

That email again is pedrazzolij@yahoo.com

The author is a very busy person so please understand that you may not get a response right away. Have patience. Thank you.

Made in the USA
Lexington, KY
25 June 2019